More Than the Blues

UNDERSTANDING DEPRESSION

by Carla Mooney

Content Adviser:
Billy AraJeJe Woods, Ph.D.,
Department of Psychology, Saddleback College,
Mission Viejo, California

Reading Adviser:
Alexa L. Sandmann, Ed.D.,
Professor of Literacy, College and Graduate School
of Education, Health, and Human Services,
Kent State University

Compass Point Books
151 Good Counsel Drive
P.O. Box 669
Mankato, MN 56002-0669

This book was manufactured with paper containing
at least 10 percent post-consumer waste.

Photographs ©: Capstone Press/Karon Dubke, cover; iStockphoto/
hartcreations, 5; Shutterstock/Tracy Whiteside, 6; Shutterstock/Monkey
Business Images, 8; Getty Images Inc./Simon Baker, 10; Aditya Kok/123RF,
12; Getty Images Inc./Dr. Dennis Kunkel/Visuals Unlimited, 15; Oscar
Williams/123RF, 16; Stephen VanHorn/123RF, 17; Shutterstock/Mandy
Godbehear, 19, 42; iStockphoto/Stockphoto4u, 20; Getty Images Inc./
Andreanna Seymore/Photonica, 21; Getty Images Inc./Christina Kennedy/DK
Stock, 23, 32; Getty Images Inc./Roy McMahon/Riser, 25; Shutterstock/Jose
AS Reyes, 26; Getty Images Inc./Mark Douet/Stone, 27; iStockphoto/motoed,
28; Shutterstock/Multiart, 30; Newscom/Tariq Zehawi/The Record/MCT, 34;
Newscom/Dean Chapple/Splash News, 37; Cathy Yeulet/123RF, 39; Elena
Kouzmina/123RF, 41.

Editor: Brenda Haugen
Page Production: Ashlee Suker
Photo Researcher: Marcie Spence
Art Director: LuAnn Ascheman-Adams
Creative Director: Joe Ewest
Editorial Director: Nick Healy
Managing Editor: Catherine Neitge

Library of Congress Cataloging-in-Publication Data
  Mooney, Carla.
  More than the blues : understanding depression / by Carla Mooney;
content adviser, Billy AraJeJe Woods; reading adviser, Alexa L.
Sandmann.
       p. cm.— (What's the issue?)
  Includes index.
  ISBN 978-0-7565-4265-8 (library binding)
  1. Depression, Mental—Juvenile literature. 2. Depression in
adolescence—Juvenile literature. I. Title. II. Series.
  RC537.M665 2010
  616.85'2700835—dc22   2009006857

Visit Compass Point Books on the Internet at *www.compasspointbooks.com*
or e-mail your request to *custserv@compasspointbooks.com*

TABLE OF CONTENTS

CHAPTER one

WHAT IS DEPRESSION?

Why can't you concentrate on anything? You know your parents are going to freak out when they see how your grades have dropped. To make matters worse, your friends are avoiding you, and your girlfriend (or your boyfriend) just broke up with you. You feel tired, but you can't sleep. You're angry and confused a lot of the time. Even your favorite pizza tastes awful these days. Everything takes too much effort. Worst of all, it seems as though there's no way to make any of it get better.

Well, listen up. You're not alone. Lots of other teens are going through the same things you are.

On the surface, Kristen* was a typical high school student. Underneath she struggled to make it through another day. "I can remember sitting at school and having teachers talk to the class or be looking at PowerPoint [presentations] to review for something important and just feel like nothing is going in and nothing made sense," she says.

Kristen's appetite disappeared, and even her favorite foods tasted bad. She found herself crying easily. Small things made her extremely irritated. She often blew up at friends and family.

Courtney couldn't escape an overwhelming sadness. "On the outside, I was a regular high school girl, but on the inside I was falling apart. I was too embarrassed to tell [friends]: 'I cry and feel sad all the time, and I don't know why,'" she says. "'I just don't think I can get through this' ran through my head every minute of every day. Whenever I

Everyone feels sad, anxious, or upset sometimes, but people with depression have symptoms that don't go away in a day or two.

* This and other names in this book have been changed for privacy reasons, except when reported in the media.

hear people say that suicide is the most selfish act of any person, I just think that they have no concept of what it's like to be depressed."

The Faces of Depression

Even though Kristen and Courtney struggle with different emotions and physical symptoms, they have the same illness—depression.

Depression is more than feeling sad or crying now and then. Lots of people feel down at times. You've probably been upset about failing a test or fighting with friends. That's perfectly normal. In fact, lots of teens talk about being depressed about problems with school or friends. Most of the time, sad feelings disappear after a few days. But what if sadness stays? When does feeling blue stop being normal and turn into a serious condition called depression?

Depression is hard to diag-

nose because it affects people differently. Like Courtney some people with depression feel sad and hopeless and lose interest in activities. Other people become extremely tired and withdraw from friends and family.

People with depression have trouble functioning in their daily lives.

Others may get into trouble. Some have trouble concentrating, sleeping, or eating. Their bodies might ache. Depression stays with you for weeks or months. It interferes with your ability to do normal activities. It affects your thoughts, feelings, and behavior.

Depression is more common than you might think. It affects as many as one in eight teens. It doesn't matter what personality you have or how successful you are at school, says Diane Stephens, a California psychotherapist. Depression can strike anyone anywhere.

As a teen, you might show depression differently than adults. In addition to being sad and tired, you might feel irri-

Facts and Figures About Depression

In the United States, depression is the most common mental health disorder.

- Twenty percent of teens experience depression.
- At any one time, 5 percent of teens are struggling with major depression.
- Depression in teens can last longer than in adults—8.3 percent of teens will suffer for at least a year, compared with 5.3 percent of adults who suffer that long.
- Depression can recur—20 percent to 40 percent have a second episode within two years, and 70 percent have a second episode before adulthood.

table, angry, or anxious. Other times you might cause problems at school and home. Especially if you're a guy, you might feel violent toward yourself or others. Judith Davenport, a California psychotherapist, believes teen depression is different from adult depression because teen minds are still developing. If you have trouble expressing your feelings, a cry for help could turn into troubling behavior and physical symptoms.

Not a Choice

If you're acting depressed, your family and friends might think you should just get over it. To them, you're being moody. It's

Depression can mess with your sleep patterns. Some people suffering from depression feel like sleeping all the time, while others have trouble sleeping at all.

Guys and Depression

Depression is not just a girl problem. Guys get depressed, too. That's not a surprise, considering guys today face a lot of stress. Some of their stresses include:

- feeling pressure to drink beer, try drugs, or have sex
- competing to be the fastest, strongest, and smartest
- balancing work and school
- dealing with parental divorce

Many guys don't learn how to manage their stress. They can have problems figuring out what's bothering them. Our society teaches guys that it's not OK to talk about feelings of sadness or confusion, says psychiatrist Michael Hunt. As a result, guys worry they'll be made fun of if they talk about how they feel. Holding all that stress inside can trigger behavior problems. In fact, guys are more likely to act violently, recklessly, and self-destructively when they're feeling stressed or depressed.

important to remember, however, that depression is not a choice. It's an illness. You can't turn it off. True depression rarely goes away on its own. Unlike bad moods that evaporate in days, depression usually tightens its grip day after day, week after week.

Major Depression

"I was tired of everything, just completely exhausted from life. It was painful for me to have to do anything, because I was so tired of it," says Claire. For a long time Claire didn't understand why she felt that way. "I tried to act normal and happy, and I just couldn't. I was crying all the time or throwing fits. Or I'd get really, really angry for no apparent reason." Finally Claire went to the doctor. His diagnosis—major depression.

Claire's condition, also known as clinical depression, is the most common form of depression. The start is often linked to a stressful event such as a family death or parental divorce. Once it triggers, you might notice your symptoms getting worse over a few weeks until you're in a full depression.

A stressful event, such as the death of a family member or friend, can bring on symptoms of depression. Don't be afraid to ask a trusted adult for help.

Depression can last for seven to nine months. You might feel irritable instead of sad. Once you have had it, you are more likely to become depressed in the future.

Dysthymia

Dysthymia is a milder form of depression. It also lasts longer than major depression—for an average of four years. Becky has this type of depression. She believes people shouldn't take it less seriously. "In my eyes, dysthymia is as bad [as major depression], if not worse," she says.

You can develop dysthymia when you are as young as 5. As a small child, you can feel sad for most of the day. After a while, you don't realize these feelings are unusual, because you've felt that way for so long. You're also more likely than people without dysthmia to become depressed again as you get older.

Bipolar Disorder

Some people have bipolar disorder, also known as manic depression. Bipolar means that moods swing between highs and lows. Manic moods can cause you to feel happy and excited. You might feel as if you were moving at hyper speed. Zack describes his first manic episode: "I thought that I was enlightened and knew the meaning of life, like I was a Buddha or Gandhi. I felt invincible, like I was on top of the world and could do anything. I even thought I had psychic powers like ESP. I didn't sleep because I felt like it was a waste of time. I stayed up all night writing poetry. I talked nonstop even though I'm usually

"I thought that I was enlightened and knew the meaning of life, like I was a Buddha or Ghandi."

quiet. I spent a thousand dollars on CDs, clothes, and food for my friends."

When the mood swings down,

11

People with bipolar disorder often enjoy the manic or up moods and decide to quit taking medication that balances their moods. But this can be dangerous.

you might feel sad and hopeless. Other times you might feel angry and irritable. It is very important to get treatment for bipolar disorder. Teens with this illness have an increased suicide risk, particu-larly during down mood swings.

In any form, depression is a serious and complicated illness. It is, however, treatable. All teens with depression can be helped.

QUIZ

Signs of Trouble

Are you or someone you know suffering with depression? If you answer yes to several of these questions, you should talk to a doctor or therapist who specializes in depression. Only a trained health professional can determine for sure whether you are depressed.

- Do you feel sad and empty?

- Is nothing fun anymore?

- Do little things make you mad?

- Do you feel tired all the time?

- Are you unhappy and bored with everything?

- Do activities you used to enjoy no longer make you happy?

- Do you feel as if people don't like you?

- Are you sleeping too much? Or too little?

- Have your eating habits changed?

- Are you having trouble concentrating?

- Do you feel as if no one understands?

- Have you been drinking or doing drugs to feel better?

CHAPTER two

WHY AM I DEPRESSED?

No one knows exactly what causes depression. Most experts believe a combination of factors influence depression. These risk factors can be genetic, biochemical, and environmental.

The Chemicals in Your Brain

Researchers are looking at how the brain works to learn about depression. Current studies show that many people with depression have a chemical imbalance in the brain. Chemicals that send signals across gaps between nerve cells are called neurotransmitters. They affect how you feel, think, and behave. Sometimes neurotransmitters such as serotonin get out of balance. This imbalance can cause the messages from your brain to your body to get jumbled. When this happens, you may experience depression symptoms.

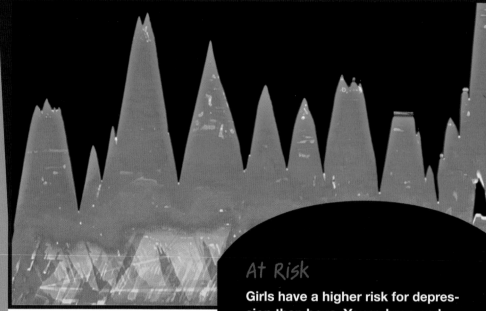

Serotonin crystals

Teens can't turn off the symptoms by themselves. Depression is a biological illness, just like asthma or diabetes.

A Family Connection

Research shows depression runs in families. Depressed teens are 20 percent to 50 percent as likely than other teens to have a family member with depression, according to the U.S. sur-

At Risk

Girls have a higher risk for depression than boys. Young boys and girls have an equal chance of becoming depressed, according to the National Institute of Mental Health. In the early teens, however, girls become depressed at twice the rate of boys.

Some experts believe the pressure girls feel to fit in increases their risk. Girls are more likely to be:

- affected by sexual harassment at school
- valued more by peers for their appearance than for their intelligence or personality
- experiencing puberty as they make a stressful change from elementary to junior high school
- physically changing early, increasing their risk for low self-esteem and depression

15

geon general. Chad knows that his family history of depression puts him at higher risk. "I'm definitely susceptible," he says. "I monitor myself, because I understand what depression is and what others in my family have gone through."

For Kristen, depression struck at 13. "Because depression runs in my family, I recognized that I had it but didn't say anything for a while because I didn't want to be … like everyone else in my family," she says. Eventually Kristen realized depression wouldn't change how her family felt about her.

Despite the family connection, no one has found a depression gene that you can inherit from your parents. Some people think that growing up in a house with depressed parents can put you more at risk. For Kristen, living with a bipolar father was stressful. "My father did not seek treatment for a lot of years for his bipolar disorder, so he went back and forth from highs to lows, and I didn't understand exactly what caused it. I always felt like I was capable of fixing things for people, so when I couldn't fix [his] depression, it bothered me," she says.

Teens with a depressed parent are three times as likely as other teens to develop depression, too.

Stressful Events

Sometimes a stressful event triggers depression. It's normal to be sad when a family member

Coping With Stress

How do you deal with stress?

1. Do you feel upset, talk it over with friends and parents, and eventually feel better? If so you probably have healthy coping skills and a good support network. This can help you avoid depression.

2. On the other hand, do you constantly blame yourself for failing? Do you hide your feelings? You may feel unable to control or change your life. You may be at risk for depression.

dies or parents divorce. When this happens, you might feel sad for a period of time but eventually rebound.

If you're depressed, you don't rebound. Your sadness or anger can grow or last longer than is normal. Janessa was 15 when her boyfriend died in an accident. "It set off a really bad depression. I didn't get out of bed. I wouldn't shower. I wouldn't eat. I felt like I was just dead,"

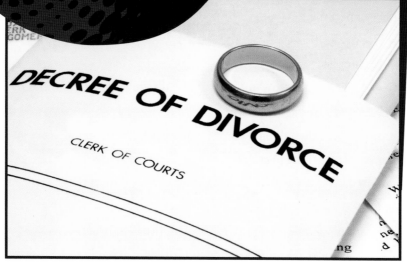

It's OK to have strong feelings if your parents are going through a divorce, but it's best to talk to someone about those feelings. If you can't talk to your parents, approach your school counselor or another trusted adult.

she says. Eight months later, she still didn't feel better.

For a teen, a problem that is minor to an adult might be a crushing blow. For some teens, the pressure to succeed and get good grades is overwhelming. Rick struggled to keep up with his brother. He says: "I've been depressed and down on myself because I can't be what my parents want me to be. My older brother was this super athlete and top student, and [my parents] think he's perfect. They expect me to be like my brother, and I can't be—and they don't think I'm any good if I can't measure up. I feel like nothing I ever do will please them or make them proud. I wonder if they really love me. And I feel pretty much alone."

Changing schools or breaking up with a boyfriend or girlfriend might also trigger stress when you're a teen. When Melanie moved with her family from New Jersey to San Francisco, she lost interest in hobbies and began sleeping a lot. Her mother took her to a therapist, who discovered that the cause of her depression was the loss of a significant person in her life— her best friend.

"I've been depressed and down on myself because I can't be what my parents want me to be."

Previous Depression and Anxiety Disorders

Sometimes your mental health history puts you at a higher risk for depression. Once you've had an episode of depression, you're more likely to become depressed again. Other mental illnesses also can increase your risk.

Anxiety disorders are a type of mental illness linked to depression. If you have an anxiety disorder, you might feel a fear or worry that overwhelms and paralyzes you. When Jodi had her first

Sources of stress at school, such as being bullied or struggling with grades, can lead to depression.

panic attack, she felt extreme fear, was short of breath, and had heart palpitations. Over a period of time, Jodi's panic attacks got more frequent and severe. Eventually she was afraid to leave her house. At that point, she developed depression symptoms.

Child Abuse

Abuse—whether verbal, physical, sexual, or emotional—can lead to depression. When Jenna was 6, her swim team coach began touching her in ways that made her feel uncomfortable. The touching continued for several years. When Jenna was 12, her family planned to go on a family canoe trip with the coach. Jenna feared the impending trip. She began to cry all the time and broke out in angry outbursts. Finally she told her parents what was bothering her. After canceling the trip, Jenna's and guilt can grow and lead to depression.

It's Hard to Be Different

Being a teen is hard. Something that makes you different can put added pressure on you. You may feel that you don't fit in with everyone. Being overweight, having a physical disability, or being gay can harm your self-esteem. Feeling bad about your differences can trigger depression.

At 10 Gayle discovered she had diabetes. A few years later, she became depressed. "I just got sick of having to be different," she says. "I couldn't eat everything my friends ate. And my parents drove me bananas with their concern. I felt for a long time like my parents sometimes used my diabetes to control me, to keep me from doing things I wanted to do." With a therapist's help, Gayle learned to accept her diabetes. "Now I feel like a normal person who just happens to have a medi-

No one has the right to abuse another person. If you're suffering from any kind of abuse, get help right away.

family immediately sought help. Her doctors diagnosed her with depression and anxiety.

Like Jenna, if you've been abused, you might feel powerless. Keeping abuse a secret can make you feel more alone and negative. As a result, feelings of self-hatred, anger, sadness,

Kids who are overweight are at risk for developing depression.

cal problem that I can control," she says. "I don't feel strange, out-of-it, and depressed that much anymore."

Having depression risk factors doesn't mean you will definitely become depressed. You should, however, take these signs seriously. Knowing that you have a higher risk of becoming depressed may lead you to ask for help sooner.

Helping to Prevent or Lessen Depression

Mental health experts have identi-fied several factors that help prevent or lessen depression. These factors help you adapt and cope when things go wrong.

- Feeling that someone cares for you
- Parents who get along with each other and expect you to get along with others, too
- Having a positive adult role model
- Having friends
- Routine and rules at home
- Parents who set clear limits but listen to your thoughts and are aware of your feelings

CHAPTER three

HOW DOES DEPRESSION AFFECT YOUR LIFE?

Depression affects your life in many ways. Emotional, behavioral, and physical changes can affect you at home and school. Relationships with friends and family may become more difficult. Depression can also lead to eating disorders, substance abuse, and cutting.

Emotional Impact

Depression wreaks havoc with your emotions. As a result, you may act differently around friends and family. "I would cry at the drop of a hat and take whatever they said personally. Sometimes I would cry for no reason and wouldn't know why," says Nicole.

If you're angry or irritable, you might pick fights with friends and family. "I am normally not an emotional person," Kristen says. "But when I am depressed I will cry

Threats of Suicide

A teen who threatens to commit suicide might be seriously depressed. Friends and parents need to listen when a teen talks about not wanting to live. Call the doctor; go to the emergency room. Other suicide warning signs include:

- giving away prized possessions
- risky or reckless behavior
- joking or romanticizing about death or suicide
- writing stories or drawing pictures about death
- listening to music about death
- visiting Internet sites about death

much easier and become extremely irritated about the most ridiculous little things and blow up on people for doing next to nothing." Sometimes that anger can even spill over into school or work.

Behavioral Impact

Depression affected Maleah's behavior. She withdrew from friends

It's normal for teens to sometimes argue with their parents, but it can also be a sign of depression.

and family. "I lost interest in everything I usually liked to do," she says. "I didn't do much of anything; mostly I would lie on my bed and stare out the window. I felt emotionally disconnected from everyone at school, and I was always tired. My friends didn't like to hang out with me because they were confused as to why I was acting this way. … I quit my [musical] instrument and found the easiest of tasks ridiculously stressful."

Isolation and losing interest in activities often happen with depression, says Elayne Savage, a therapist who treats teens with depression.

Or you might have trouble concentrating. You might pace, become overly involved in activities, and be unable to relax. For Kristen, this restless behavior signaled depression. "Everyone pretends like people who are depressed lay in bed and do nothing, but I almost always end up the opposite … running around in my room doing anything I can to occupy myself and keep myself from thinking about all the things that bother me."

Behavior changes may be difficult for parents and friends to understand. "My parents weren't sure how to deal with what was going on," Maleah says. "When I started acting odd, my mother would try to comfort me or tell me I could go into another room for a while. My father would get really uncomfortable and would sit silently, waiting for me to ride it out."

"I didn't do much of anything; mostly I would lie on my bed and stare out the window. I felt emotionally disconected from everyone at school, and I was always tired."

Risky Behavior

For some teens, depression leads to risky decisions and misbehavior. Getting into fights, running away, skipping class, using drugs and alcohol, cutting yourself, and having sex can all be signs you're in a serious depression. Misbehavior often happens when a teen can't cope with feelings of depression. For many, it is an attempt to escape depression.

Kara, diagnosed with bipolar disorder at age 16, turned to alcohol to help her cope with depression. "I would use alcohol to hide my emotions. I ended up drinking a lot. ... It would help for a little bit, but then would make it worse." Kara eventually decided to stop drinking. "It wasn't worth it anymore. It wasn't fun."

Some teens such as Kristen choose to avoid risky behavior. "I can't say that I haven't thought of it ... drinking, drugs, cutting. But I have never turned to them as a solution to my problem," she says.

Teens who are depressed may turn to drugs as a solution, but it only adds to their problems.

25

"I guess because I have seen too many people my age turn to risky behavior to take their mind off how depressed they are, and I've seen the outcome; they don't end up any happier."

Physical Effects

Depression also can affect you physically.

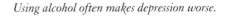

Using alcohol often makes depression worse.

Changes in sleep patterns are common. Kara says, "I would get super tired. I needed a lot of sleep. It would wipe me out completely." Others, such as Melissa, develop insomnia. "I would put [sleep] off for hours because I knew that once I lay down I would never get to sleep anyway," she says. "This caused me to be tired all the time."

Depression can also affect how you eat. Some people lose interest in food and lose weight.

Depression affects people in different ways. You might feel tired and sick or often have headaches. A doctor can help you discover whether you're suffering from depression or another health problem.

Depression can change your appetite.

just want to sit around and eat," says Chad.

Depression can cause headaches, stomachaches, back pain, and a general feeling of tiredness. Kara would get bad migraines when depressed. "Standing up hurt," she says. "My head just hurt."

Becky experienced severe stomach pains. When gastric tests came back negative, Becky began seeing a therapist. Within a few months, her stomach pains disappeared. "What is clear to me now is that my stomach serves as a gauge of my emotional well-being. When I

One of the biggest things Kristen noticed about her depression was her appetite change. "When I am really depressed, I barely eat or what I eat just tastes nasty to me." Others eat compulsively and gain weight. "When I feel down, I get tired and hungry. I really have no energy at all, and I

"When I am really depressed, I barely eat or what I eat just tastes nasty to me."

have stomach pains or digestive problems, it usually means that too many things have built up."

CHAPTER four

FINDING HELP AND GETTING BETTER

Depression is a treatable disease. Most teens respond well to treatment and return to a normal life. Early diagnosis and treatment, however, are very important. Untreated depression can become serious and linger for months.

The First Step— Asking for Help

If you suspect depression, what should you do? The first step toward feeling better is asking for help. "The biggest tip I can give a teen that is depressed and wants to tell someone is just to tell them," Kristen says. "Sit down and make a list of the different ways that you could say it. Rehearse it if you feel like you need to. Chances are the people closest to you have probably already noticed that you haven't been acting like yourself lately."

Start with Mom or Dad. Sit down in a quiet place when you both have time to talk. Explain how you've been feeling and say you need help to feel better.

If you don't want to talk to your parents, don't give up. Try reaching out to another trusted adult who can help you get treatment. Talk to a school counselor, family doctor, or social worker.

If you aren't getting help from your parents or other adults, reach out to a 24-hour telephone hotline. The trained staff will help you find treatment.

Sometimes you might feel too sad or hopeless to ask for help. If this happens, your friends and family can help you get treatment. During Maleah's freshman year of high school, she would cry uncontrollably. Her mother noticed her becom-

The first step to feeling good again is to ask for help.

ing increasingly disconnected from her family. "At that point I needed medical attention. My mother brought me in to our doctor, and she suggested a therapist," Maleah says.

Most teens don't get help for depression. Many teens deny their depression, says therapist Elayne Savage. They are afraid to tell anyone about their feelings, and others might have trouble recognizing the signs. "Most teens don't even know, really, what depression is, so how can they ask for help?" asks Chad. "I'm lucky, in a way, in that I've seen it firsthand in my family, so I'm probably more aware than the average teen and could ask someone close to me for help." For other teens, the stigma of mental illness stops them from getting treatment. They feel embarrassed. They don't see depression as a medical condition.

Maleah agrees that teens can be slow to get help. "It took me

Facts About Treatment

- **Fewer than 33 percent of teens with depression seek help.**
- **Doctors and therapists can successfully treat 80 percent of teens with depression.**
- **The leading cause of suicide is untreated depression. Suicide is the third leading cause of death for teens, after accidents and homicide.**

a while to agree to therapy," she says. "I didn't feel I needed it."

Being a guy might also make you less likely to ask for help.

"It took me a while to agree to therapy. I didn't feel I needed it."

Many boys learn at a young age to tough it out and take care of themselves. As a result, they often don't ask for help. They

Talking with a therapist regularly helps many people deal with depression.

don't want to seem weak. Daniel admits that he first tries to work it out himself. "If that [doesn't] work, I talk to my mom or sister," he says.

Get an Evaluation

When you do decide to get help, you will first be evaluated by a health professional. Jenna felt overwhelmed at her evaluation. "You're hearing all of this terminology that sounds abso-

lutely terrible. … I was nervous just because you are talking to someone you don't know about deep, personal feelings."

At the evaluation the expert will look for any illnesses or medications that might be causing your symptoms. He or she will also want to know:

- How often do your symptoms occur? How long do they last?
- Is there a family history of depression?

Who Treats Depression?

Many types of health professionals treat people with depression.

- **Primary care doctors are often involved in the initial diagnosis. They may also refer you to a mental health specialist.**
- **Psychiatrists are medical doctors who diagnose and treat depression. They can write prescriptions and also provide talk therapy.**
- **Psychologists have doctoral degrees in psychology. They can diagnose depression and are trained in talk therapy.**
- **Nurse practitioners are nurses with advanced training. They can diagnose depression, prescribe medication, and provide talk therapy.**
- **Clinical social workers can diagnose depression and provide talk therapy.**

- How are things at home and school?
- Are you using alcohol or drugs?
- Have you had thoughts of suicide?

Kristen remembers being nervous before her first therapist visit. "I was scared to talk about certain feelings I had. … I didn't know what to say at first, but I think that she picked up on that and did most of the talking, making me feel much more comfortable. She told me a little bit about herself, too, which made it feel more personal."

If the health professional finds you have depression, he or she will develop a treatment plan. The plan could include talk therapy, medication, hospitalization, or a combination of these things.

Talk Therapy

In talk therapy, a depressed person talks to an expert about his or her feelings and problems. These talks can happen in one-on-one sessions, with family members, or in a group setting. During therapy sessions, you learn to recognize and change unhealthy thoughts and behaviors. Talk therapy can help you feel more in control of your life.

"Learning to express my emotions when I have them and not holding them in for months and then breaking down has been one of the most important things I have learned," says Kristen. You might feel uncomfortable talking about problems and feelings. Honest talks with a therapist, however, can be quite

Some teens benefit from one-on-one therapy, group therapy, or therapy with a parent. Some benefit from two or all three approaches.

effective. "Therapy is by far the most helpful treatment to me because it always is without judgment and is a very cathartic place," Jenna says.

Sometimes patients and therapists build long-term relationships. "I have seen my therapist now for six years," Kristen says. "We still talk, and I love her as if she were a part of my family; she even came to my high school graduation."

Beyond Therapy— Medicine

Sometimes you might need more than talk therapy to feel better. In these serious cases, a doctor may prescribe depression medicine, called antidepressants.

Depression medicines are not

Talk Therapy

The most common types of talk therapy are cognitive-behavioral therapy and interpersonal therapy. CBT tries to change your negative views of yourself, the world, and the future. First you identify negative thoughts and behaviors. Then you work to make them more positive and productive. Studies show that CBT is one of the most effective types of depression therapy.

IPT focuses on relationships with others. This therapy helps people understand how interacting with others makes them feel. It will help you learn strategies to get along better with family and friends.

a quick fix. They usually take at least a month to start working. In addition, not all medicines work for everyone, and some people experience side effects. Nicole's doctor prescribed several medicines before finding the right combination for her. "It has been difficult for me at times to take my medication. However, as every day passes, I realize how important it is to take your medication and how it has helped me through a lot of difficult times," she says.

Taking medicine every day and dealing with side effects, such as nausea, weight gain, and sleeplessness, isn't always fun. Even though you want to stop taking your medicine as soon as you feel better, don't do it. This can be a big mistake and may allow depression to return.

While medicine is not a cure-all, it can help you get on the path to feeling better. "Medication helped me get stable enough to

THE STEWART AND LYNDA RESNICK
NEUROPSYCHIATRIC HOSPITAL AT UCLA
760 WESTWOOD

In some cases, such as when a teen is in danger of hurting himself or herself, hospitalization is necessary.

deal with my emotions and talk about my feelings," Kara says.

Hospitalization

Some depressed people may need to stay in a hospital. This can happen if depression gets worse in spite of talk therapy or medicine. In the hospital, doctors and nurses watch patients closely. In addition, the hospital has intense therapy for people with serious depression.

At 16 Kara talked about killing herself. Her worried mother and doctor admitted her to the hospital. There Kara spent a few days until she was well enough to leave. Then she transferred to an outpatient treatment program.

Whether treatment is talk therapy, medicine, or a hospital stay, there is hope. Most people have happy and successful lives after treatment for depression.

CHAPTER five

MOVING FORWARD

Depression doesn't have to ruin your life. With treatment and support, it's possible to live a full and happy life. The support of family and friends, as well as certain lifestyle changes, can help keep depression away.

Finding Support

One key to beating depression is getting support. Often this comes from trusted friends or family members. You might find support from people who also have depression. It can be hard to ask for help, but no one should have to face depression alone.

For many, family is the best source of support. Kara relies on her mother and brother. "They were always there to talk to me. It would help because I felt really alone," she says. Her family pushed her to keep doing the things she liked to do.

Other people find support outside their family. Melissa relies on several friends. "My friends help because they're there on a day-to-day basis and they know me. They can tell when I'm depressed and trying to hide it from them. They know when to not let me go ... when to take away things that could be used to hurt myself."

She also talks to a few trusted adults who are role models for her. "They lived through it, and they're the way that I can look and see [that] they went through this too, and they made it ... they're always there to listen and give their advice."

Learn About Depression

Knowledge is power. The more you learn about depression, the better you'll be able to understand and cope with it. Knowledge helps you understand why you feel a certain way and why a treatment plan works. Bookstores and libraries have many books on depression. In

Spending time with good friends can be great therapy, too.

Don't Abandon Treatment

Treatment isn't an instant fix. Beating depression takes hard work over a long period of time. There will be times when going to therapy isn't convenient. When they feel better, some teens think they can stop treatment entirely. That decision shouldn't be made alone. Doctors, therapists, and family members need to be involved in making treatment changes.

Years after her diagnosis, Kristen still battles with depression and continues treatment. "The most important thing that I have to tell myself when I begin feeling depressed is ... well, that I'm depressed. Recognize it and don't let it consume your life, because it will if you stand by and allow it to," she says.

Be Good to Yourself

Exercising, eating right, and getting enough sleep are all ways to

addition, mental health facilities and nonprofit groups have brochures, Web sites, and seminars about depression and its treatment.

help your body stay in balance. Exercise has the added benefit of releasing chemicals called endorphins into the brain. Endorphins are a natural way to lift mood and boost energy. Jenna uses exercise to release stress. "If you force yourself to work out, the change in your mood [for the better] is dramatic," she says.

Sleep allows the body to rest and cope with the stresses of everyday life. It builds up energy for another day. Without enough sleep, you may feel tired and cranky. You may also be more vulnerable to depression.

Reduce Stress

Managing stress is an important step toward a happy and healthful life. Over the years Jenna learned to deal with stress through writing and art.

Other ways to reduce stress include:

- Simplify. Cut back on activities.

- Stay positive. Try to find the good things in every situation. Avoid negative thoughts that lead to hopelessness and anxiety.
- Recognize warning signs. Learn what triggers stress and depression symptoms. Make a plan to cope with triggers before they happen.

Playing sports can help you feel better physically and emotionally.

Finding Hope

After years of struggling with depression, Kara finally seems to be reaching a happier place. She has kicked her alcohol habit and no longer talks about killing herself. With the support of her family and therapists, she's finding her place in a new school, making friends, and getting back into life. She still gets waves of depression, but she has figured out how to handle them before the depression gets too bad. She says: "I used to take everyone's problems and my own and keep them bottled up. [I've learned that] I have to look out for myself. If I talk to people and get it out of myself, the depression goes away." Kara has another piece of advice for teens: "If you have depression, don't try to cure it yourself."

Kara's experience shows that education, treatment, and support can lead to hope. Perhaps Maleah sums it up best when she says, "Nothing should have to block you from feeling happy."

Many people do yoga to help relieve stress.

QUIZ

Ways to Help Yourself

Are you on the right track to keep depression away? Take this quiz to see whether you've got the tips down cold. True or false—you can fight depression by:

1. meditating to release stress

2. talking to your family and friends about what is bothering you

3. skipping your therapy appointment because you've got too much homework

4. taking a walk around the block

5. drinking beer to have a good time

6. adding more activities to your already overscheduled calendar

7. writing in a journal

8. getting eight hours of sleep each night

Answers: 1. True 2. True 3. False 4. True
5. False 6. False 7. True 8. True

GLOSSARY

anxious   feeling worried, nervous, or afraid

cope   face and deal with problems

diagnose   determine what is making a person sick

genetic   related to genes that are passed from parents to children

insomnia   not being able to fall sleep or stay asleep

interferes   gets in the way or becomes an obstacle

irritable   easily annoyed

serotonin   brain chemical related to depression

stigma   undesirable mark or trait

therapy   treatment of a disease or problem

WHERE TO GET HELP

Depression and Bipolar Support Alliance
730 N. Franklin St., Suite 501
Chicago, IL 60610
800/826-3632
The Depression and Bipolar Support Alliance is a nonprofit organization that provides hope, help, and support to people with depression or bipolar disorder. It can help you find a support group in your area and get educational materials to learn about mood disorders.

Families for Depression Awareness
395 Totten Pond Road
Waltham, MA 02451
781/890-0220
Families for Depression Awareness is a nonprofit organization that helps families recognize and cope with depressive disorders.

Mental Health America
2000 N. Beauregard St., 6th Floor
Alexandria, VA 22311
703/684-7722
hotline: 800/273-8255
Mental Health America is a nonprofit organization dedicated to helping people live mentally healthy lives. It can help you learn about depression and other mental health disorders through education programs.

National Alliance on Mental Illness
2107 Wilson Blvd., Suite 300
Arlington, VA 22201
703/524-7600
The National Alliance on Mental Illness is a nonprofit organization that has affiliates in more than 1,100 communities across the country. NAMI works to improve the lives of those affected by mental illness.

SOURCE NOTES

Chapter 1

Page 5, column 1, line 4: Kristen. Fort Smith, Ark. E-mail interview. 18 July 2008.

Page 5, column 2, line 5: Maureen Empfield and Nicholas Bakalar. *Understanding Teenage Depression.* New York: Henry Holt, 2001, p. 17.

Page 9, column 2, line 2: Kathiam M. Kowalski. "Dealing With Depression—Beyond the Blues." 24 March, 2008. *Current Health 2*, December 1999, p. 6.

Page 11, column 1, line 13: *Understanding Teenage Depression*, p. 40.

Page 11, column 2, line 11: Families for Depression Awareness. "Zack and Nancy." 31 March 2009. *www.familyaware.org/familyprofiles/nancyzack0.php?pid=2*

Chapter 2

Page 16, column 1, line 3: Chad. San Diego, Calif. E-mail interview. 21 Dec. 2008.

Page 16, column 1, line 10: Kristen.

Page 16, column 2, line 14: Kristen. E-mail interview. 8 Sept. 2008.

Page 17, line 10: Lisa Machoian. *The Disappearing Girl: Learning the Language of Teenage Depression.* New York: Penguin, 2005, p. 103.

Page 18, column 1, line 9: Kathleen McCoy. *Understanding Your Teenager's Depression.* New York: Berkley, 2005, p. 28.

Page 20, column 2, line 15: Ibid., p. 40.

Chapter 3

Page 22, line 16: Nicole. Boston, Mass. E-mail interview. 14 Aug. 2008.

Page 22, line 23: Kristen, E-mail interview. 18 July 2008.

Page 24, column 1, line 1: Maleah. Syracuse, N.Y. E-mail interview. 19 July 2008.

Page 24, column 1, line 26: Kristen.

Page 24, column 2, line 9: Maleah.

Page 25, column 1, line 16: Kara. Madison, Wis. Telephone interview. 14 Aug. 2008.

Page 25, column 2, line 2: Kristen. E-mail interview. 8 Sept. 2008.

Page 27, column 1, line 2: Kara.

Page 27, column 1, line 6: Melissa. Milwaukee, Wis. E-mail interview. 18 July 2008.

Page 28, column 1, line 3: Kristen. E-mail interview. 18 July 2008.

Page 28, column 1, line 8: Chad.

Page 28, column 2, line 8: Kara.

Page 28, column 2, line 17: *Understanding Teenage Depression*, p. 36.

Chapter 4

Page 29, line 14: Kristen. E-mail interview. 8 Sept. 2008.

Page 31, column 1, line 2: Maleah.

Page 31, column 1, line 13: Chad.

Page 31, column 1, line 28: Maleah.

Page 32, column 1, line 2: Daniel. Chicago, Ill. E-mail interview. 8 Jan. 2009.

Page 32, column 1, line 10: Jenna. Dallas, Texas. E-mail interview. 8 Sept. 2008.

Page 33, column 1, line 9: Kristen.

Page 34, column 2, line 2: Kristen. E-mail interview. 18 July 2008.

Page 35, column 1, line 1: Jenna. E-mail interview. 23 July 2008.

Page 35, column 1, line 8: Kristen. E-mail interview. 8 Sept. 2008.

Page 36, column 1, line 8: Nicole.

Page 36, column 2, line 13: Kara.

Chapter 5

Page 38, line 19: Ibid.

Page 39, column 1, line 3: Melissa.

Page 40, column 2, line 18: Kristen.

Page 41, column 1, line 7: Jenna. E-mail interview. 8 Sept. 2008.

Page 42, column 1, line 17: Kara.

Page 42, column 2, line 5: Maleah.

Fiction

Brown, Susan Taylor. *Hugging the Rock*. Berkeley: Tricycle Press, 2006.

Burtinshaw, Julie. *Adrift*. San Diego: Raincoast Books, 2002.

Fritz, April Young. *Waiting to Disappear*. New York: Hyperion, 2002.

Holmes, Sara. *Letters From Rapunzel*. New York: HarperCollinsPublishers, 2007.

Young, Janet Ruth. *The Opposite of Music*. New York: Atheneum Books for Young Readers, 2007.

Nonfiction

Cobain, Bev. *When Nothing Matters Anymore: A Survival Guide for Depressed Teens*. Minneapolis: Free Spirit Publishers, 2007.

Miller, Alan R. *Living With Depression*. New York: Facts on File, 2007.

Schab, Lisa M. *The Anxiety Workbook for Teens: Activities to Help You Deal With Anxiety & Worry*. Oakland: Instant Help Books, 2008.

Zucker, Faye, and Joan E. Huebl. *Beating Depression: Teens Find Light at the End of the Tunnel*. New York: Franklin Watts, 2007.

Internet Sites

FactHound offers a safe, fun way to find Internet sites related to this book. All of the sites on FactHound have been researched by our staff.

Here's all you do:
Visit *www.facthound.com*
FactHound will fetch the best sites for you!

INDEX

ABOUT THE AUTHOR

Carla Mooney lives in Pittsburgh, Pennsylvania, with her husband and three children. She received her bachelor's degree in economics from the University of Pennsylvania. She works as a freelance writer and has written several books and articles for young readers.

ABOUT THE CONTENT ADVISER

Billy AraJeJe Woods has a doctorate in psychology, a master's degree in education, and a bachelor's degree in psychology. He has been counseling individuals and families for more than 25 years. He is a certified transactional analysis counselor and a drug and alcohol abuse counselor. A professor of psychology at Saddleback College, Mission Viejo, California, Woods teaches potential counselors to work with dysfunctional families and special populations. He began his counseling career in the military, where he worked with men and women suffering from post-traumatic stress disorder. In his practice, Woods has worked with many young adults.